WITHDRAWN

LOUISVILLE
CARDINALS

BY MARTY GITLIN

Published by ABDO Publishing Company, PO Box 398166, Minneapolis, MN 55439. Copyright © 2014 by Abdo Consulting Group, Inc. International copyrights reserved in all countries. No part of this book may be reproduced in any form without written permission from the publisher. SportsZone™ is a trademark and logo of ABDO Publishing Company.

Printed in the United States of America,
North Mankato, Minnesota
072013
092013

 THIS BOOK CONTAINS AT LEAST 10% RECYCLED MATERIALS.

Editor: Chrös McDougall
Series Designer: Craig Hinton

Photo Credits: Darron Cummings/AP Images, cover, 7; David Longstreath/AP Images, 1, 26; Atlanta Journal Constitution, Curtis Compton/AP Images, 4; MCT/ZUMA Press/Icon SMI, 9; David J. Phillip/AP Images, 10; Kevin McGloshen, News and Tribune/AP Images, 12; Gerald Herbert/AP Images, 16, 42 (top left); AP Images, 18, 25, 31, 42 (top right); Bettmann/Corbis/AP Images, 21; William P. Straeter/AP Images, 23, 43 (top middle); Harold Filan/AP Images, 28; Brian Horton/AP Images, 33, 42 (bottom middle); Ron Heflin/AP Images, 34, 43 (bottom left); Tom Strickland/AP Images, 37; Laura Rauch/AP Images, 39; Chris Steppig/NCAA Photos/AP Images, 41, 43 (bottom right); Shutterstock Images, 44

Design elements: Matthew Brown/iStockphoto

Library of Congress Control Number: 2013938131

Cataloging-in-Publication Data
Gitlin, Marty.
 Louisville Cardinals / Marty Gitlin.
   p. cm. -- (Inside college basketball)
Includes index.
ISBN 978-1-61783-916-0
1. University of Louisville--Basketball--Juvenile literature. 2. Louisville Cardinals (Basketball team)--Juvenile literature. I. Title.
796.323--dc23

2013938131

TABLE OF CONTENTS

Louisville coach Rick Pitino, *right*, hugs forward Chane Behanan after the Cardinals won the 2013 national title.

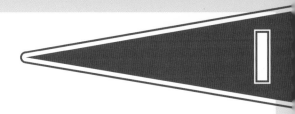

TERRIFIC TEAM TITLE

THE DATE WAS APRIL 26, 2013. THE CITY WAS LOUISVILLE, KENTUCKY. THE PLACE WAS A TATTOO PARLOR. UNIVERSITY OF LOUISVILLE CARDINALS MEN'S BASKETBALL COACH RICK PITINO WAS ABOUT TO ENTER. HIS MISSION? TO GET A TATTOO THAT HE HAD NEVER WANTED.

It all started on February 9, 2013. His team had just lost in five overtimes to the Notre Dame Fighting Irish. His players were tired and frustrated. To lift their spirits, he told them that they were going to win the rest of their games. He predicted that they would snag the Big East Conference Tournament title, make the National Collegiate Athletic Association (NCAA) Tournament, and reach the Final Four.

Pitino then changed the subject. He said the players needed to stop getting so many tattoos. The players then asked Pitino if he would get his own tattoo if they won the national title. He agreed.

CARDINALS

Nearly three months later, Pitino was getting that tattoo. It featured the words "2013 NCAA Champions." Pitino had been right. The Cardinals had not lost another game. They had won their last 16 games to capture the crown.

The first 14 wins were easy. Louisville won 13 of them by eight points or more. Eight were against teams ranked in the top 25 in the country. Among them was a shocking 85–63 blowout of the second-ranked Duke Blue Devils. That victory sent the top-ranked Cardinals into the Final Four.

However, that game was also remembered for a devastating injury. Late in the first half, Louisville sophomore guard Kevin Ware landed awkwardly as he contested a shot. His right foot twisted when it hit the floor. His leg was shattered, and TV cameras captured the whole thing. Ware's teammates grimaced and clutched each other when they saw Ware crumble in pain in front of their bench. The game

stopped. Players from both teams were in emotional agony. Some prayed for him.

The Cardinals were inspired to win the title for their fallen friend. But first they had to get past the red-hot Wichita State Shockers. Wichita State was a ninth seed. That made the Shockers only the fifth team in tournament history to reach the Final Four with a seed of nine or lower. Ware was on the sideline in crutches and a cast when his team played. And with 13 minutes left in the game, he was frustrated. Louisville was trailing 47–35, and he could not do anything about it.

TERRIFIC TEAM TITLE

Suddenly, junior guards Luke Hancock and Tim Henderson caught fire. Henderson, forced into action because of Ware's injury, nailed two three-pointers. Hancock drove to the basket for two layups. The Shockers' lead was down to 50–45. Hancock later hit a three-pointer to put Louisville ahead 56–55 with 6:31 remaining.

Hancock then delivered the knockout blows. He first drilled another three-pointer with just over two minutes left. And then he scored on a layup 52 seconds later to give the Cardinals a 67–62 lead. Soon they were celebrating a 72–68 victory.

The job was not complete, though. The Michigan Wolverines stood in Louisville's way of a national title—and a tattoo for Pitino. Ware was proud of the way his teammates came back to shock the Shockers. But he knew it would mean nothing unless they beat the surging Wolverines.

"We've got to bring our best game," Ware said. "It's the last game of the season. If we lose, everything we've worked for just goes down the drain. That's the last thing we want right now."

A HORSE TALE

Louisville coach Rick Pitino likes to honor his players. So he names the racehorses he owns after them. The first horse he named after a player was Gorgui (Gorgui Deng). The next were Siva (Peyton Siva) and Russdiculous (Russ Smith). He then turned over the job to horse trainer Dennis O'Neill. O'Neill created the name Three Point Luke in honor of 2013 NCAA Tournament hero Luke Hancock.

Louisville's Luke Hancock drives against Wichita State during the 2013 Final Four.

Ware would not be disappointed. New heroes were about to emerge for the Cardinals. Sophomore forward Chane Behanan made two foul shots with 13:50 left. That gave his team the lead at 49–47. His tip-in of a missed shot stretched it to 54–49. Senior guard Peyton Siva attacked the basket with abandon. He scored 10 points on layups

and dunks during a six-minute stretch. Hancock then clinched the championship. His three-pointer with 3:27 to go put the Cardinals ahead 76–66. It was all over but the celebration.

The final score was Louisville 82, Michigan 76.

When the final second ticked off the clock, Ware and Pitino received more hugs from teammates than anyone. This was not the most talented roster Pitino had ever coached. These Cardinals won because they played team basketball. That was what made this moment so special.

"We have a brand where it's Louisville first, everything for the team," Pitino said. "It's tough to recruit players with that total attitude, but they bought in and I'm real proud of them."

The winning tradition of Louisville basketball had continued. But the team had suffered through a lot of losing before that winning tradition began.

SUPER SUB

Junior guard Luke Hancock was named the 2013 Final Four's Most Outstanding Player. That was no surprise. Hancock played a key role in the semifinal win over Wichita State. He then scored 22 points in the title-clinching defeat of Michigan. He hit all five of his three-point attempts in that game. What was surprising was that Hancock was not even a starter for the Cardinals. He was the first reserve to earn that honor in the 75 years the event had been played.

TERRIFIC TEAM TITLE

The University of Louisville was founded in 1846 in Louisville, Kentucky.

MOSTLY BAD BASKETBALL

THE FIRST LOUISVILLE MEN'S BASKETBALL GAME WAS NOT GLAMOROUS. IN FACT, THAT GAME IN 1912 WAS A 35–3 LOSS TO A TEAM REPRESENTING THE LOUISVILLE YMCA.

William Gardiner had agreed to coach the team. It was a thankless job. The Cardinals played just three games in their first year and lost them all, scoring just 23 points in the process.

Soon college basketball began thriving in the state of Kentucky. Louisville began a storied rivalry with the Kentucky Wildcats in 1913. The two teams now meet every season. Russ Brown, author of *Cardinals Handbook*, expressed the passion many of the state's people have for college basketball.

"Basketball is special to Kentuckians," he wrote. "[It] permeates everyday life from offices to farms, from coal mines to neighborhood drug stores. It is more than just a sport played in the cold winter months. It is a source of

BIRTH OF A PROGRAM

Louisville got a late start in basketball. Many other schools in the area already had teams when the Cardinals were born in 1912. Included was the University of Kentucky, known then as State College. The Wildcats had begun play in 1903.

The city of Louisville was thriving by 1900. It rests beside a stretch of Ohio River rapids. It served as a link for the transport of goods from the eastern part of the United States to the West. The growth of the city made it an ideal spot for the sport to take hold. Organized games were played in YMCA and church leagues in Louisville as early as 1895.

The University of Louisville did not field a men's team until 17 years later. Even when the Cardinals began play they had no home court. They were forced to host games at nearby Tharp Business School.

pride and a year-round cause for anticipation, hope, and celebration."

Winning, however, was not a source of pride at Louisville until after World War II. Gardiner quit after one season. The Cardinals had losing records every year until 1916. A lack of money caused further problems. It prevented Louisville from even sporting a team in 1917 and 1923. The Cardinals played without a coach from 1913 to 1915. And no coach remained in place for more than two seasons until Tom King guided the squad from 1925–26 to 1929–30.

The Louisville team featured little talent and depth in its early days. In 1917–18, forward Sam Morgan averaged 17.3 points per game. That was a school record that stood for 23 years. But Louisville still stumbled to just a 3–4 mark. Morgan scored 121 points that season. The other players tallied just 32 points combined.

Louisville enjoyed four straight winning seasons from 1926–27 to

1929–30 without a standout player. No one on those teams averaged more than eight points per game. But forwards Fred Koster and Eddie Weber plus guards Jim Blackerby, Ed "Froggy" Craddock, and Bennie McDonald provided skill and depth.

The departure of coach King brought inconsistent play and many coaching changes. Louisville did not again record back-to-back winning seasons until the mid-1940s. Weber replaced King in 1931 and led the team to a 15–7 record the following year. But that success was short-lived.

The Cardinals began playing opponents from outside of Kentucky under new coach C. V. "Red" Money. In 1934, they set a school record by winning 16 games in one season. Little did Louisville fans suspect that they were about to face the darkest period in program history.

The struggles began when Lawrence Apitz was hired as coach in 1935–36. The Cardinals sported an 8–19 record combined during the next two years—and then got even worse. They finished just 1–15 in 1938–39 and 1–18 in 1939–40.

FIGHTING, NOT PLAYING

A large number of Cardinals joined the US effort in World War II from the start. As such, Louisville did not even boast enough players to field a team for the 1942–43 season. Many of the players joined the Navy. So when the team did return to the court the following year, its name was changed to the Sea Cards. That was done to honor those who fought in that branch of the service.

MOSTLY BAD BASKETBALL

Their only victories those two years were achieved against tiny Berea College of Kentucky. That prompted *Louisville Courier-Journal* writer Larry Boeck to joke, "In Louisville's case, instead of 'God Bless America' it should be 'God Bless Berea.'"

By 1942 the United States was involved in World War II. Young men throughout the nation were sent overseas to fight. Included were University of Louisville athletes. World War II changed the United States forever. Cardinals basketball also would never be the same. The program was about to blossom into one of the finest in the country.

Coach Peck Hickman guides the
Louisville Cardinals during a 1947 game.

WINNING AND MORE WINNING

WORLD WAR II WAS STILL RAGING IN EUROPE AND ASIA IN 1944. THE BATTLES WOULD CONTINUE INTO 1945. BUT MANY OF THE YOUNG MEN WHO SURVIVED THE FIGHTING WERE RETURNING HOME. ON THE BASKETBALL COURT, THE CARDINALS WERE READY TO BEGIN A NEW ERA.

They needed a fresh start. They had not enjoyed a winning season in eight years. Louisville athletic director John Heldman was fretting over the program. He thought the school might even lose its men's basketball team.

Few gave it a second thought when an unknown named Peck Hickman was chosen to coach the team. He had never coached college basketball. But Heldman felt so strongly about his candidate that he told Hickman he was needed to save the Cardinals.

The Hickman era began with a bang. Louisville clobbered Georgetown College 99–27 in his first game. It was the largest point total in team history and a record that would stand for nine years. The 72-point margin of victory remained the biggest ever for the Cardinals through 2013. Louisville won its first seven games that season and finished with a 16–3 record.

The Cardinals had begun a run of 46 straight winning seasons. They captured a secondary tournament championship in 1948. That capped a season in which the team won a school-record 29 games. The Cardinals earned their first trip to the NCAA Tournament in 1951 but lost in the first round to archrival Kentucky.

At that time, the National Invitation Tournament (NIT) in New York was as important as the NCAA Tournament. The Cardinals began making annual appearances in the NIT. They participated every year from 1952 to 1956.

Louisville captured the NIT title in the last of those seasons behind center Charlie Tyra. The 6-foot-8 Tyra had blossomed into the finest player in Louisville history to that point. He set a school record by

GREAT CARDINAL, AVERAGE KNICK

Center Charlie Tyra was one of the greatest players in Louisville basketball history. But his talent did not translate into National Basketball Association (NBA) stardom. Tyra was drafted by the Fort Wayne Pistons and traded to the New York Knicks. He played four years with the Knicks and one with the Chicago Packers. He never averaged more than 12.8 points and 8.1 rebounds per game. Some believe Tyra, a Louisville native, felt uncomfortable in the spotlight of a big city such as New York.

Louisville's Bob Lochmueller attempts to block a shot against Western Kentucky during the 1952 NIT.

averaging 23.8 points per game in 1956. He led the team that year to a 26–3 mark, its best ever at the time. And he averaged more than 20 rebounds per game in his last two seasons.

Sports Illustrated writer Billy Reed praised Tyra after the Cardinals' star died in 2006. "No player in [school] history has ever worked harder than Tyra," Reed wrote. "Quiet to the point of shyness off the floor, he led by example. He never quit. He never stopped working."

Neither did Hickman. His 1959 Cardinals had no player as great as Tyra, but they heated up in the NCAA Tournament. The tournament was much smaller back then. No more than 25 teams took part until it expanded to 32 in 1975. The tournament has featured at least 64 teams each year since 1985.

In 1959, the Cardinals won their first game to set up a Sweet 16 date against Kentucky. But their hope of becoming the first Louisville team to reach the Final Four was in jeopardy when they fell behind by 15 points. Hickman screamed at his players at halftime. He believed they were intimidated by the Wildcats' rich tradition.

"You know what's beating you?" he fumed. "Those [darn] blue uniforms. You can beat this team if you forget all that 'Big Blue' tradition [stuff]. But if you keep playing like this, you might as well join them and put on blue ones, too."

WONDERFUL WES

Wes Unseld went on to a great career in the NBA after leaving Louisville. Despite being short for a center at 6-foot-6, he proved to be one of the finest rebounders in league history. Unseld was named the NBA's Most Valuable Player and Rookie of the Year in 1969. He averaged more than 10 rebounds per game 12 times. He also played in five All-Star Games and helped the Washington Bullets win the 1978 NBA title.

The inspired Cardinals roared back to upset the second-ranked Wildcats. Louisville then beat the Michigan State Spartans to steamroll into the Final Four. More exciting was that the Cardinals were hosting the event at home in Freedom Hall.

But one young man on a great team stood in their way. That was brilliant guard Jerry West, who led the West Virginia Mountaineers. West scored 27 points in the first half against the Cardinals. The Mountaineers rolled to a 94–79 victory over Louisville, but then lost to the California Golden Bears in the final.

WINNING AND MORE WINNING

GRANTING A WISH

Mulley Goldberg might have been the Louisville Cardinals' biggest fan in 1959. His son played for the Louisville freshman team. But the elder Goldberg was dying of cancer. He had been attending home games but was now too weak. He had listened to the first-round NCAA Tournament win over the Eastern Kentucky Colonels on the radio. And he vowed to find the strength to watch the second-round showdown against the Kentucky Wildcats in person.

As the team celebrated that victory, Cardinals player Don Goldstein asked two ushers to lift Goldberg out of his seat. They hoisted him onto the court to join the festivities. Tears of emotion ran down his cheek. "You gave me one last thrill and I want to thank you so much," he told Goldstein. "I felt like maybe you were playing for me out there." Goldberg died less than a month later.

The bubble had burst for Louisville, which had been the surprise team of the tournament. A line in the *Louisville Courier-Journal* the next day used a fairy tale reference to mark the end of a dream season. "Cinderella came home a bit early from the ball last night," it read.

The Cardinals continued to win through the 1960s. They featured one of the premier players in the sport in Wes Unseld. The burly 6-foot-6 center averaged more than 20 points per game during his last three years. He later earned a spot in the Naismith Memorial Basketball Hall of Fame after a stellar NBA career.

The Louisville teams of that decade also boasted high-scoring guard Butch Beard, a future NBA All-Star. The Cardinals earned NCAA Tournament berths in 1961, 1967, and 1968. But they could not advance past the second round in any of those years.

Hickman retired in 1967 to become the school's athletic director. John

Louisville's Butch Beard shoots against a Fordham player during the 1969 NIT in New York City.

Dromo replaced him as coach. But that did not last long. Dromo left soon after having a heart attack after a game. Denny Crum took over the coaching duties in 1971–72. A new era of greatness was about to begin.

Louisville coach Denny Crum, shown in 1986, helped the Cardinals rise to national prominence.

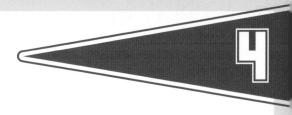

FROM CONTENDER TO CHAMPION

DENNY CRUM KNEW WHAT IT TOOK TO WIN AS AN
ASSISTANT COACH AT THE UNIVERSITY OF CALIFORNIA,
LOS ANGELES (UCLA). DURING HIS TIME THERE, THE UCLA BRUINS
WERE THE GREATEST DYNASTY IN COLLEGE BASKETBALL HISTORY.
JOHN WOODEN WAS PERHAPS THE GREATEST HEAD COACH EVER.
CRUM DREAMED OF SOMEDAY REPLACING HIM.

But it was the dream of Louisville athletic director Peck
Hickman to bring a championship to his own school. He
did not achieve that goal as coach despite great success. He
understood how tough it was to win a title. So he interviewed
Crum before the 1971–72 season and came away impressed.
The feeling was mutual. Crum put aside his desire to coach at
UCLA and took the Louisville job.

The team Crum took over was not as talented as the
teams from the 1960s. It did have some good players, though.
Sharp-shooting guard Jim Price averaged 21 points per game
that season. And when the NCAA Tournament began, the

Louisville's Al Vilcheck, *right*, and UCLA's Bill Walton battle for a loose ball during their 1972 Final Four game.

Cardinals were ready. They rolled through their first two games. That made Crum the first rookie head coach to reach the Final Four.

His reward was a showdown against Wooden and his powerful UCLA team. The Bruins had not only won five straight titles, they also boasted one of the greatest players ever in center Bill Walton. Crum had recruited nearly all the players to UCLA. Now he would be forced to create a plan to beat them.

But no plan was good enough to stop Walton. The 6-foot-11 redhead dominated with 33 points and 21 rebounds. The result was a 96–77 Bruins victory over the Cardinals. Louisville forward Henry Bacon summed up the defeat simply.

"Our guys could play with their guys," he said. "Except they had Bill Walton. No one else did. Some of our guys didn't have good games. He had a perfect game."

The Bruins no longer had Walton for their rematch against Louisville in the 1975 Final Four. Meanwhile, the Cardinals were loaded with talent. Included was future NBA star swingman Junior Bridgeman. Louisville averaged more than 81 points per game that season. The team scored more than 100 three times. Then it won its first three NCAA Tournament games by an average of 14 points.

GETTING ALL WET

Cardinals players began a "war of water" during their 1980 title run. They began dumping buckets of ice water on each other. The fun got out of hand at a hotel in Lincoln, Nebraska. Senior guard Tony Branch heard a knock on his door and assumed it was a teammate. He opened the door and dumped a bucket of ice water on the visitor. Little did he know that the visitor was coach Denny Crum. Crum did not get angry. Instead, he waited several days and dumped a bucket of ice water on Branch.

Many believed the 1975 UCLA-Louisville game would be more competitive than the previous game. They were right. The dramatic semifinal reached overtime. The Cardinals led by one point with three seconds left. They needed only to make both ends of a one-and-one to reach the finals for the first time. But the Bruins' Marques Johnson rebounded the missed free throw and teammate Richard Washington nailed a jump shot to win the game. Final score: UCLA 75, Louisville 74.

The Cardinals were crushed. But they would get another chance to beat UCLA in the 1980 NCAA championship game. All was not well at halftime in that game, however. Louisville was losing by two points. And Crum was not happy.

He spoke to the team in the locker room. Two stinging words stood out from that speech: "You're choking," he said.

Crum would not allow his players to throw away their season. Their record was 32–3. They had enjoyed an 18-game winning streak.

ONWARD AND UPWARD

Darrell Griffith was the second overall pick in the 1980 NBA Draft. He averaged 20 points per game for the Utah Jazz in his first five seasons. But he was not the only player from the 1980 Louisville championship team to make a mark in the NBA. Rodney McCray was a solid starting player in the NBA for 10 years. Derek Smith averaged 24 points per game in the NBA in 1984–85, but his career was cut short by injuries. And Jerry Eaves and Scooter McCray—Rodney's older brother—also had short stints in the NBA.

Senior guard Darrell Griffith was a leader for the Cardinals during the 1979–80 season.

And they had steamrolled into the finals. Now they began mounting a comeback.

The Bruins held a 50–45 lead with six minutes left, but Louisville refused to stop trying. Things looked bleaker when UCLA forward Kiki Vandeweghe stole a pass and dribbled down the court for a sure dunk.

PLAYING FOR A FRIEND

Cardinals star Darrell Griffith did not want to win the 1980 NCAA title just for himself and his teammates. He also was thinking about a boyhood buddy named Jerry Stringer. Stringer had bone cancer in his hip. Griffith was asked about his friend during a press conference the day before the championship game.

"Jerry's in the third quarter and he's losing," Griffith said. "I pray to God he'll win. Hey, Jerry, tomorrow night's for you."

Stringer had been weakened by his illness, but he had enough strength to watch the game. Griffith helped cut down the nets from the baskets on the court after the Cardinals beat the UCLA Bruins. He gave Stringer one of the nets the next day as a gift. Stringer died one month later.

But Cardinals sophomore guard Jerry Eaves sprinted after him. He forced Vandeweghe to miss the shot.

Louisville grabbed the momentum and ran away with it. Star senior guard Darrell Griffith showed why he was among the finest talents in the country. He scored on a three-point play. He hit a jump shot from the corner. He twice passed to Eaves for baskets. And with the game tied, he launched a long shot from 20 feet.

Swish! The Cardinals led by two points and pulled away for a 59–54 victory. They were the champions of college basketball.

Griffith averaged 22.9 points per game that season. He was clearly the best player on the team. But he refused to hog the spotlight. Instead, he gave credit to everyone who made the dream-come-true possible.

"This was never the Darrell Griffith Show," he said. "This was the Louisville Show."

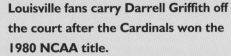

Louisville fans carry Darrell Griffith off the court after the Cardinals won the 1980 NCAA title.

Many players contributed to that victory. Among them were sophomore forward Derek Smith and freshman big man Rodney McCray. They helped turn the Cardinals into perennial contenders. The Cardinals qualified for the NCAA Tournament every year from 1981 to 1984. They reached the Final Four in 1982 and 1983 but lost to the Georgetown Hoyas and then the Houston Cougars. Another title, however, was right around the corner.

FROM CONTENDER TO CHAMPION

[33]

Louisville star Pervis Ellison (43) passes the ball against Duke during the 1986 NCAA championship game.

ONE MORE CELEBRATION

A NEW CORE OF GREAT TALENT HAD MADE ITS MARK IN LOUISVILLE BY 1986. SENIOR FORWARD BILLY THOMPSON AND SENIOR GUARD MILT WAGNER WERE ALREADY STARS. BUT IT WAS FRESHMAN CENTER PERVIS ELLISON THAT TOOK THE COLLEGE GAME BY STORM. HE AVERAGED 13.1 POINTS, 8.2 REBOUNDS, AND 2.4 BLOCKED SHOTS PER GAME IN HIS FIRST SEASON.

The Cardinals were on fire offensively in the NCAA Tournament. They scored at least 82 points in each of their first five games. They rolled into the finals against the top-ranked Duke Blue Devils. And Louisville boasted a 16-game winning streak heading into the game.

Despite his youth, Ellison was not afraid to take control against the Blue Devils. Opportunity struck with 38 seconds left. Ellison grabbed a rebound and popped it into the basket to give the Cardinals a 68–65 lead. He then made two foul shots to clinch the victory. That set off a celebration on the court and in the streets of Louisville. The Cardinals were once again national champions.

That ended up being the high point for several years in Louisville. Crum stayed on at the school for another 15 seasons. But he was never able to guide another team back to the Final Four. In 1990–91, the Cardinals suffered through their first losing season in 49 years. They rebounded to qualify for the NCAA Tournament the next six seasons. But they fell to just 12–20 in 1997–98 and 12–19 in 2000–01. They were heading in the wrong direction.

Crum resigned after the 2000–01 season. The school turned to Rick Pitino to replace him. Pitino hesitated when asked to coach the Cardinals. After all, Pitino had spent eight years coaching bitter rival Kentucky. He had even won a national title with the Wildcats. Pitino also was offered the coaching job at Michigan that same year. But his wife Joanne tried to convince him to go to Louisville.

MOVING AROUND

The Cardinals were part of the Missouri Valley Conference (MVC) from 1964–65 through 1975. They played in the Metro Conference from 1975–76 to 1994–95. Then they were in Conference USA until 2005 before joining the Big East. They gained their greatest league success in the MVC and Metro. They won or shared the MVC title six times in 11 years. They won the Metro title 12 times in 20 seasons. Louisville won its only Conference USA title in 2005, and the Cardinals won two Big East titles. In 2012, the Cardinals announced plans to move to the Atlantic Coast Conference (ACC) starting in 2014.

Louisville's Dwayne Morton drives against Delaware during the 1993 NCAA Tournament.

"I think that you love the state of Kentucky," she told him. "You love the people you met at [the school]. I think you should go back to the place you love."

Many Louisville fans and players yearned for Pitino to take the job. They did not care that he had coached at Kentucky. And soon their wish

CARDINALS

LOUISVILLE VS. KENTUCKY

The rivalry between the Louisville Cardinals and the Kentucky Wildcats heated up after they began meeting every year in 1983. And it was already pretty hot. Through 2012–13, the Wildcats owned a 30–15 all-time record against the Cardinals, including a 21–12 mark since 1983. But the intensity of the rivalry extends far beyond wins and losses.

"The national attention paid to what in reality should have been strictly a local rivalry is a testament to the outstanding coaches and players of both schools who achieved great things . . . and made the rivalry what it is today," reads a story on Big Blue History, a website dedicated to University of Kentucky basketball. "The high level of success and accomplishment is a great source of pride within the [state of Kentucky]."

In the 33 games played between the teams since 1983, both teams have been ranked in the top 20 in the nation 14 times.

was granted. "Now it's time to lead the Cardinals back to prominence," Pitino said.

The Cardinals needed a boost. They sported a 62–62 record over the previous four seasons. They had finished with a terrible 12–19 mark the previous year.

Pitino was a fiery coach who loved three-point shooters and a fast-paced style. He won 19 games and coached his team into the NIT in his first season. He made the Cardinals into title contenders again the next season, in 2002–03. They sprinted out to an 18–1 record and won an NCAA Tournament game for the first time since 1997. Then they bolted to a 16–1 mark in 2003–04 before slipping.

In 2005, the Cardinals played their best basketball in the postseason. Their run appeared over when they fell behind by 20 points to the West Virginia Mountaineers in the Elite Eight. But Pitino refused to allow his team to lose.

"I looked at Coach, and he's been in that position before," said junior guard Taquan Dean. "He told us to stay calm. We're still going to stay in this game."

They did more than stay in the game. They caught West Virginia and won 93–85 in overtime. Louisville reached the Final Four for the first time since 1986.

The Cardinals continued to fly. They returned to the Elite Eight in 2008. They rolled over their first three opponents by an average of 22 points. But standing in their way of another Final Four appearance was the powerful North Carolina Tar Heels. And Louisville was forced to attempt an upset at a "neutral" court in Charlotte, North Carolina.

ONE MORE CELEBRATION

The Cardinals fell behind by 12 points before staging a comeback to forge a 59–59 tie. However, North Carolina pulled away in the final minutes to win.

Senior forward Juan Palacios was not complaining. He understood that his teammates were expected to watch most of the NCAA Tournament from their televisions at home. Their run to the doorstep of the Final Four was a surprise.

"We couldn't hang our heads," Palacios said. "[North Carolina] could have beaten us by 25 or 30 points like they've been doing to other teams, but we came back and it was a tough game. We've got to be proud of ourselves that we were able to come back and give them a game."

The Cardinals returned to a familiar spot in 2009. They won 13 games in a row, including a stunning 103–64 victory over the Arizona Wildcats in the Sweet 16. A win over the Michigan State Spartans would put Louisville back in the Final Four. But the Cardinals made just 18 baskets the entire game and were outscored 17–7 during one stretch

THE FIRST TO THREE FINAL FOURS

Rick Pitino became the first coach in history to guide three different schools to the Final Four. He coached the Providence Friars to the semifinal round in 1987. He took the Kentucky Wildcats there in 1993, 1996, and 1997. Then he led the Cardinals to the Final Four in 2005, 2012, and 2013. He boasted an overall coaching record of 662–235 through 2012–13.

Louisville guard Peyton Siva dunks against Michigan during the 2013 NCAA championship game.

in the second half. They simply did not play well enough to beat the Spartans, who rolled to the title.

Louisville could not make it past the first round of the 2010 and 2011 NCAA Tournaments. But the Cardinals soared to the Final Four in 2012 and won it all for the third time in 2013. It had become apparent that Pitino was true to his word when he was hired in 2001. He had indeed brought Cardinals basketball back to prominence.

TIMELINE

The Cardinals play their first game on January 28 and lose to the Louisville YMCA 35–3.

The Cardinals complete their first winning season with a 53–15 win over Centre on March 2.

Tom King takes over as coach and becomes the first to guide the Cardinals for more than two seasons.

Peck Hickman is hired as coach and transforms the program into one of the finest in the country.

The Cardinals qualify for the NCAA Tournament for the first time but fall in the first round on March 20 to the archrival Kentucky Wildcats 79–68.

1912   1916   1925   1944   1951

Crum becomes the first rookie head coach to take his team to the Final Four. The Cardinals fall to the UCLA Bruins 96–77 in the semifinals on March 23.

The Cardinals again lose to UCLA in the Final Four, this time 75–74 in overtime, on March 29.

Louisville clinches its first NCAA title, gaining revenge against UCLA with a 59–54 victory in the finals on March 24.

The Cardinals again reach the Final Four but fall to the Georgetown Hoyas 50–46 in the semifinals on March 27.

Louisville steamrolls into the Final Four for the third time in four years but drops a 94–81 decision in the semifinals to the Houston Cougars on April 2.

1972   1975   1980   1982   1983

Center Charlie Tyra plays his first season with Louisville. He becomes one of the best Louisville players of all time.

Louisville clinches its first NIT title with a 93–80 triumph over the Dayton Flyers on March 24.

The Cardinals win an NCAA Tournament game for the first time, defeating the Eastern Kentucky Colonels 77–63 on March 10.

Center Wes Unseld begins his career with the Cardinals and becomes one of the finest players in school history.

Denny Crum replaces John Dromo as Louisville coach.

1954   1956   1959   1965   1971

The Cardinals capture their second NCAA crown in seven years with a 72–69 defeat of the Duke Blue Devils on March 31.

Louisville finishes with a 14–16 record for its first losing season since World War II.

Crum retires and Rick Pitino takes over as coach of the Cardinals.

The Cardinals reach the Final Four for the first time since 1986 but fall to the Illinois Fighting Illini in the semifinals 72–57 on April 2.

Louisville wins its first NCAA title in 27 years on April 8 with an 82–76 victory over the Michigan Wolverines.

1986   1991   2001   2005   2013

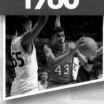

QUICK STATS

PROGRAM INFO
University of Louisville Cardinals
   (1912–)

NCAA TOURNAMENT FINALS
(WINS IN BOLD)
1980, 1986, 2013

OTHER ACHIEVEMENTS
Final Fours: 10
NCAA Tournaments: 39
Conference titles: 22

KEY PLAYERS
(POSITION(S); YEARS WITH TEAM)
Butch Beard (G; 1966–69)
Junior Bridgeman (G-F; 1972–75)
Jack Coleman (F; 1946–49)
Pervis Ellison (C; 1985–89)
Reece Gaines (G; 1999–2003)
Francisco Garcia (F; 2002–05)
Darrell Griffith (G-F; 1976–80)
George Hauptfuhrer (C; 1944–46)
Allen Murphy (G-F; 1972–75)
Jim Price (G; 1969–72)
John Reuther (F-C; 1962–65)

Derek Smith (F; 1978–82)
John Turner (F; 1958–61)
Charlie Tyra (C; 1953–57)
Wes Unseld (C; 1965–68)
DeJuan Wheat (G; 1993–97)

KEY COACHES
Denny Crum (1971–2001):
   675–295 (42–23 NCAA Tournament)
Peck Hickman (1944–67):
   443–183 (5–7 NCAA Tournament)
Rick Pitino (2001–):
   310–111 (22–9 NCAA Tournament)

HOME ARENA
KFC Yum! Center (2010–)

* All statistics through 2012–13 season

After a two-point loss to the Eastern Kentucky Colonels in 1956, angry Louisville coach Peck Hickman met his wife outside the locker room. "Oh, come on, Peck," she said. "It's not all that bad. You still have the two girls and me." "Yeah," he replied. "But right now, I'd trade all three of you for three [darn] points."

Coach Peck Hickman left his senior players in charge of making dinner plans before a 1959 game against Kentucky. He warned them to keep the expenses down. Instead, the seniors ordered steaks, baked potatoes, corn on the cob, and apple pie. They then presented assistant coach John Dromo with the huge bill. "You guys have to beat Kentucky now," Dromo said. "Because when [Hickman] sees this, he's gonna kill all of you and then fire me!"

Center Wiley Brown, who played for Louisville's 1980 national title team, had one of his thumbs amputated after a childhood accident. Louisville team physician Rudy Ellis and trainer Jerry May devised a plastic thumb that fit over Brown's stub. That helped him grip the ball. One day Brown left his plastic thumb at a restaurant and forgot about it. Coach Denny Crum sent freshman Randy Bufford into a dumpster near the restaurant to find it. Bufford found it under some eggs.

GLOSSARY

conference
In sports, a group of teams that plays each other every season.

draft
A system used by professional sports leagues to select new players in order to spread incoming talent among all teams. The NBA Draft is held each June.

dynasty
A team that wins several championships in a short period of time.

postseason
The tournaments that take place after the regular season and conference tournaments, including the NIT and the NCAA Tournament.

recruit
To secure the services of a player to join a college basketball team.

rival
An opponent that brings out great emotion in a team, its fans, and its players.

rookie
Somebody in their first year.

seed
In basketball, a ranking system used for tournaments. The best teams earn a number-one seed.

upset
A result in which the supposedly worse team beats the supposedly better team.

FOR MORE INFORMATION

FURTHER READING

Brown, Russ. *Cardinals Handbook*. Wichita, KS: The Wichita Eagle and Beacon Publishing Company, 1996.

DeCock, Luke. *Great Teams in College Basketball History*. Chicago, IL: Heinemann-Raintree, 2005.

Gigliotti, Jim. *College Basketball Guide: All the Teams, All the Stars, All the Big Games*. Santa Barbara, CA: Beach Ball Books, 2010.

WEB LINKS

To learn more about the Louisville Cardinals, visit ABDO Publishing Company online at **www.abdopublishing.com**. Web sites about the Cardinals are featured on our Book Links page. These links are routinely monitored and updated to provide the most current information available.

PLACES TO VISIT

College Basketball Experience
1401 Grand Boulevard
Kansas City, MO 64106
816-949-7500
www.collegebasketballexperience.com

This interactive museum allows visitors to experience various aspects of college basketball. It also includes the National Collegiate Basketball Hall of Fame, which highlights the greatest players, coaches, and moments in the history of college basketball.

KFC Yum! Center
1 Arena Plaza
Louisville, KY 40202
502-690-9090
www.kfcyumcenter.com

The Cardinals moved into this arena in November 2010. A number of events aside from college basketball games, such as rock concerts, are held here.

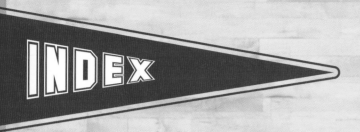

INDEX

ABOUT THE AUTHOR

Marty Gitlin is a freelance writer based in Cleveland, Ohio. He has had more than 70 educational books published. Gitlin has won more than 45 awards during his 25 years as a writer, including first place for general excellence from the Associated Press. He lives with his wife and three children.